Keys, Legends, and Symbols in Maps

JULIA J. QUINLAN

PowerKiDS
press
New York

Published in 2012 by The Rosen Publishing Group, Inc.
29 East 21st Street, New York, NY 10010

First Edition

Editor: Amelie von Zumbusch
Book Design: Greg Tucker

Photo Credits: Cover, pp. 4–5, 8–9, 10–11, 14–15, 16, 17 © GeoAtlas; pp. 5 (inset), 9 (inset), 13, 15 (inset), 18 (inset), 22 Shutterstock.com; pp. 6–7, 20–21 © United States National Parks Service; p. 12 © Riccardo Pravettoni, UNEP/GRID-Arendal, http://maps.grida.no/go/graphic/carbon-stored-by-biome; pp. 18–19 © U.S. Geological Survey.

Library of Congress Cataloging-in-Publication Data

Quinlan, Julia J.
  Keys, legends, and symbols in maps / by Julia J. Quinlan. — 1st ed.
     p. cm. — (How to use maps)
  Includes index.
  ISBN 978-1-4488-6154-5 (library binding) — ISBN 978-1-4488-6266-5 (pbk.) —
ISBN 978-1-4488-6267-2 (6-pack)
  1. Map reading—Juvenile literature. 2. Maps—Symbols—Juvenile literature. I. Title.
  GA130.Q48 2012
  912.01'48—dc23
                                        2011017725

Manufactured in the United States of America

CPSIA Compliance Information: Batch #WW12PK: For Further Information contact Rosen Publishing, New York, New York at 1-800-237-9932

Contents

Understanding Symbols

Maps are helpful tools that people use to travel and to learn about different places. Most maps have **symbols**, or pictures, on them that show important **features**. These features include capital cities, rivers, and roads.

Many maps use the same symbols. For example, a star may show where a

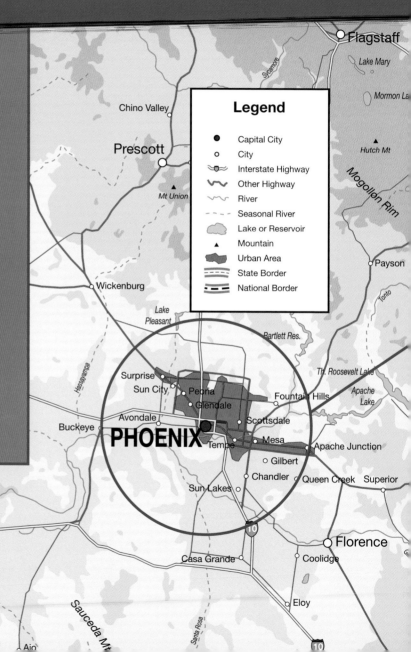

Legend

- ● Capital City
- ○ City
- Interstate Highway
- Other Highway
- River
- Seasonal River
- Lake or Reservoir
- ▲ Mountain
- Urban Area
- State Border
- National Border

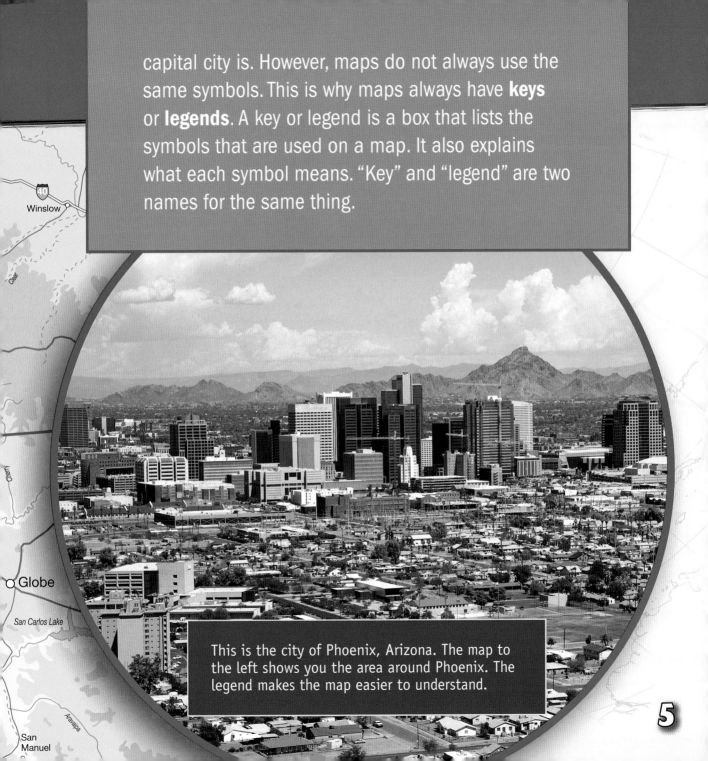

capital city is. However, maps do not always use the same symbols. This is why maps always have **keys** or **legends**. A key or legend is a box that lists the symbols that are used on a map. It also explains what each symbol means. "Key" and "legend" are two names for the same thing.

This is the city of Phoenix, Arizona. The map to the left shows you the area around Phoenix. The legend makes the map easier to understand.

5

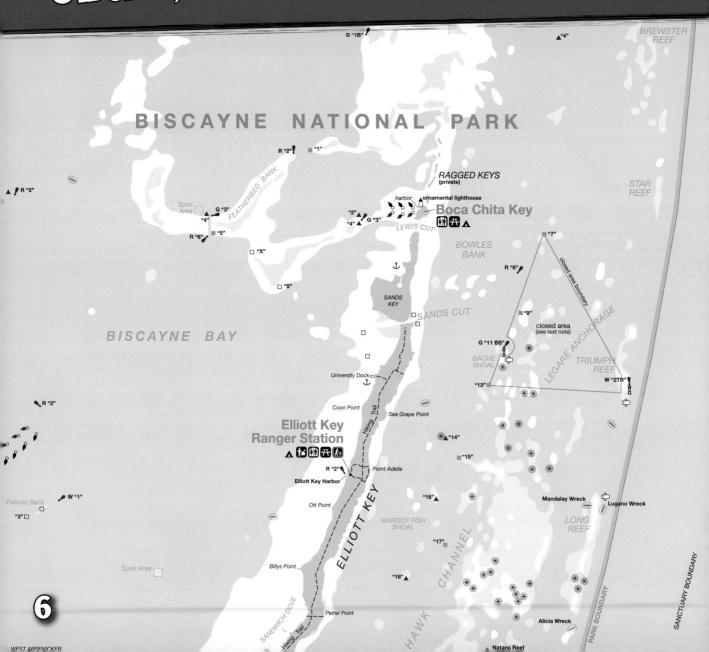

PARK BOUNDARY

Y "C"

R "2"

G "1B"

▲"4"

BREWSTER REEF

BISCAYNE NATIONAL PARK

R "2" ▪ "1"

RAGGED KEYS
(private)

STAR REEF

FEATHERBED BANK

Spoil Area

G "3"

"4" ▲

R "6" ▪ "5"

▪ "X"

harbor   ornamental lighthouse

Boca Chita Key

"2"

"4" ▲ G "3"

LEWIS CUT

▲ R "2"

BOWLES BANK

▪ "7"

R "8"

closed area boundary

LEGARE ANCHORAGE

TRIUMPH REEF

▪ "9"

closed area
(see text note)

▪ "S"

SANDS KEY

⚓

SANDS CUT

BISCAYNE BAY

G "11 BS"

BACHE SHOAL

"13"

W "2TR"

University Dock

Coon Point

Hiking Trail

Sea Grape Point

**Elliott Key
Ranger Station**

▲ "14"

R "2" ▲

R "2"   Point Adelle

Elliott Key Harbor

▪ "15"

Ott Point

ELLIOTT KEY

"16" ▲

Mandalay Wreck

Lugano Wreck

LONG REEF

Pelican Bank

W "1"

"2" ▢

MARGOT FISH SHOAL

HAWK CHANNEL

Spoil Area

Billys Point

"17"

"18" ▲

SANDWICH COVE

Petrel Point

Hiking Trail

Alicia Wreck

SANCTUARY BOUNDARY

PARK BOUNDARY

WEST ARSENICKER

Natans Reef

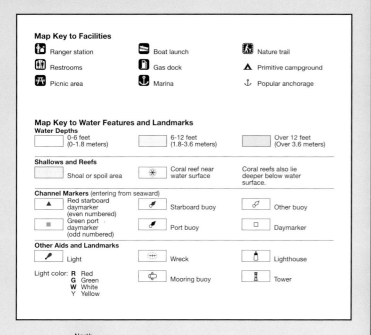

Map Key to Facilities

🏚	Ranger station	🛥	Boat launch	🏞	Nature trail
🚻	Restrooms	⛽	Gas dock	▲	Primitive campground
⛱	Picnic area	⚓	Marina	⚓	Popular anchorage

Map Key to Water Features and Landmarks

Water Depths

0-6 feet (0-1.8 meters)	6-12 feet (1.8-3.6 meters)	Over 12 feet (Over 3.6 meters)

Shallows and Reefs

Shoal or spoil area	✳ Coral reef near water surface	Coral reefs also lie deeper below water surface.

Channel Markers (entering from seaward)

▲	Red starboard daymarker (even numbered)	🖌	Starboard buoy	◺	Other buoy
■	Green port daymarker (odd numbered)	🖌	Port buoy	□	Daymarker

Other Aids and Landmarks

🖌	Light	⊕	Wreck	🗼	Lighthouse
Light color:	R Red	⊕	Mooring buoy	🏛	Tower
	G Green				
	W White				
	Y Yellow				

North

↑

0	2 Kilometers	
0	2 Statute Miles	
0	2 Nautical Miles	

Scale

Stars, circles, dots, and even forks are called point symbols. Point symbols help us find places on a map. On a map of the United States, all major cities would be marked with a point symbol. Many maps use bigger dots for bigger cities.

A map of a city might have pictures of forks on it. On many maps, a fork shows where a restaurant is. There is a symbol for almost anything you can think of! To find out what each symbol means, look at the key or legend.

This is part of a map of Biscayne National Park, in Florida. Look at the point symbols in the key. Can you use the key to find a ranger station on the map?

Streets, Rivers, and Railroads

Point symbols show us where places are. Line symbols can show us how to get there! Roads, rivers, and railroads are all shown using line symbols. Different types of lines are used, though, so that we can tell these different things apart. There are even different lines used for a neighborhood street

Maps use line symbols to show rivers. This makes it easy to follow a river's path. Can you figure out which river the city of Jackson, Mississippi, is on?

Physical Map of Mississippi

Legend

- ● Capital City
- ○ City
- River
- Lake or Reservoir
- Urban Area
- State Border
- Marshlands

Russellville
Morrilton
Conway
Searcy
Lake Dardanelle
Petit Jean

Clarksdale
Enid Lake
Skuna
Aberdeen Lake
Aberdeen
Grenada Lake
Yalobusha
Yalobusha
Grenada
Big Sunflower
Tibbee
West Point
Columbus Lake
Cleveland
Starkville
Columbus
Winona
Aliceville Lake
Greenwood
Black Belt
Indianola
Noxubee
Greenville
Deer
Yazoo
Physical Map of Mississippi
Yazoo City
Philadelphia
Lake Providence
Big Black
Canton
Jackson Prairie
Okatibbe Lake
Ross Barnett Res.
Chunky
Meridian
Mississippi
JACKSON
Forest
Buckatunna
Tallulah
Brandon
Vicksburg
Bayou Macon
Strong
Tensas
Laurel
Waynesboro
Bayou Pierre
Southern Pine Hills
Natchitoches
Natchez
Bogue Chitto
Pearl
Hattiesburg
Buffalo
Columbia
Black Creek
Mississippi
Red Creek
Pascagoula
Sam Rayburn Res.
Biloxi
Wolf
Jasper 8
Bundick Lake
Bundick
Ville Platte
Mississippi
New Roads
Covington
Gulfport
Biloxi
Atchafalaya
Port Allen
BATON ROUGE
Bay St. Louis
Cat I.
Opelousas
Ship I.

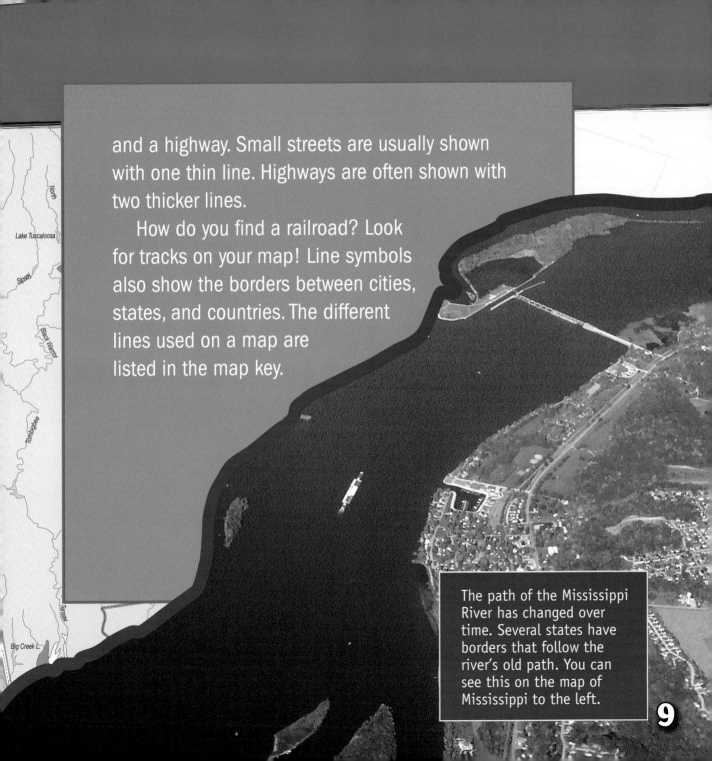

and a highway. Small streets are usually shown with one thin line. Highways are often shown with two thicker lines.

How do you find a railroad? Look for tracks on your map! Line symbols also show the borders between cities, states, and countries. The different lines used on a map are listed in the map key.

The path of the Mississippi River has changed over time. Several states have borders that follow the river's old path. You can see this on the map of Mississippi to the left.

North
Lake Tuscaloosa
Sipsey
Black Warrior
Tombigbee
Tensaw
Big Creek L.

Colorful Maps

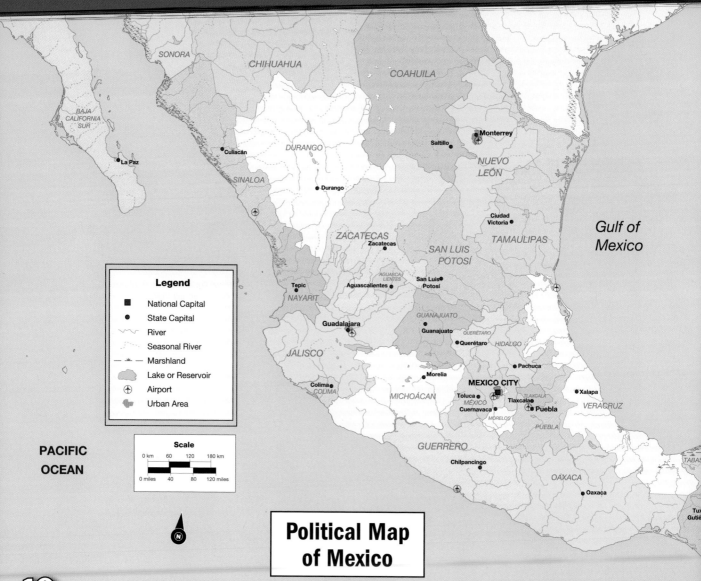

Legend

- ■ National Capital
- ● State Capital
- River
- Seasonal River
- Marshland
- Lake or Reservoir
- Airport
- Urban Area

Scale

0 km 60 120 180 km

0 miles 40 80 120 miles

PACIFIC
OCEAN

**Political Map
of Mexico**

SONORA

CHIHUAHUA

COAHUILA

BAJA
CALIFORNIA
SUR

• La Paz

• Culiacán

• Monterrey

• Saltillo

NUEVO
LEÓN

DURANGO

SINALOA

• Durango

ZACATECAS

Zacatecas

• Ciudad
Victoria

TAMAULIPAS

Gulf of
Mexico

SAN LUIS
POTOSÍ

AGUASCA-
LIENTES

Tepic

Aguascalientes

San Luis
Potosí

NAYARIT

GUANAJUATO

Guadalajara

Guanajuato

QUERÉTARO

Querétaro

HIDALGO

JALISCO

• Pachuca

Colima

Morelia

MEXICO CITY

• Xalapa

COLIMA

MICHOÁCAN

Toluca

MÉXICO

Tlaxcala

TLAXCALA

VERACRUZ

Cuernavaca

Puebla

MORELOS

PUEBLA

GUERRERO

Chilpancingo

OAXACA

TABAS

Oaxaca

Tux
Gutié

This political map of Mexico shows its states in different colors. Like many political maps, it reuses colors. States that are next to each other are never the same color, though.

Maps can have many colors. Some colors often stand for the same thing. A blue area often shows where water is. Green often shows parks or forests. Yellow or brown can show where a desert is.

Some maps have even more colors. Maps of the ocean may have different shades of blue, which show how deep the water is. Maps that show different countries will often make each country its own color. A map of the United States might have each state a different color. This helps us see where one state ends and another begins.

Many Kinds of Maps

Not all maps show cities and countries. Some maps show you natural areas, such as **biomes**. Biomes are places that share the same weather patterns and plant types. A biome map can show you where to find a rain forest, **tundra**, or desert. Each biome is marked with its own color.

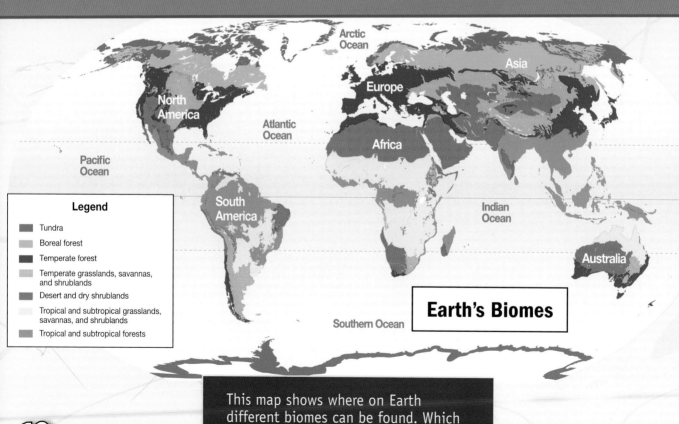

Legend

- Tundra
- Boreal forest
- Temperate forest
- Temperate grasslands, savannas, and shrublands
- Desert and dry shrublands
- Tropical and subtropical grasslands, savannas, and shrublands
- Tropical and subtropical forests

Arctic Ocean

Asia

Europe

North America

Atlantic Ocean

Africa

Pacific Ocean

South America

Indian Ocean

Australia

Southern Ocean

Earth's Biomes

This map shows where on Earth different biomes can be found. Which biome do you live in?

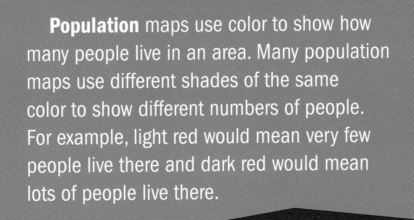

Population maps use color to show how many people live in an area. Many population maps use different shades of the same color to show different numbers of people. For example, light red would mean very few people live there and dark red would mean lots of people live there.

Polar bears live on tundra. Tundra has short summers and long, cold winters. Few trees grow there. Can you find tundra on the map to the left?

Big Word, Big Deal

Most maps are not just made up of symbols and colors. Many maps also have words, such as the names of cities, streets, and important places on them. On most maps, the bigger a word is, the more important it is. For example, the name of a capital city is often bigger than the name of a small town. City and town names are usually written in black.

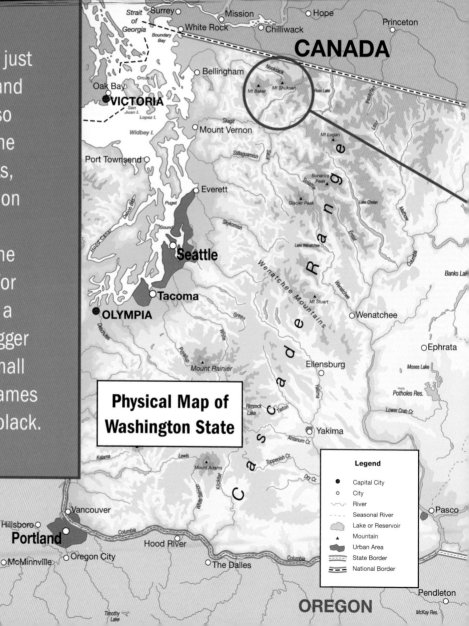

Physical Map of Washington State

Legend

●	Capital City
○	City
∿	River
- - -	Seasonal River
🔵	Lake or Reservoir
▲	Mountain
	Urban Area
▦	State Border
▦	National Border

Important features are sometimes in bold or in capital letters. Names of rivers and oceans are often in blue and in **italics**, or slanted letters. Sometimes words on a map are **abbreviated**, or shortened. "SP" often stands for "state park."

Mount Shuksan, seen here, is in northwest Washington. As you can see, its name is abbreviated as Mt Shuksan on the physical map of Washington to the left.

Which Way and How Far

Knowing which way is which is important for understanding maps. Most maps have **compass roses**. The compass rose shows which way is north, south, east, and west.

Another useful tool is a **scale bar**. Maps show smaller versions of real places. Scale bars help us understand how far apart things on

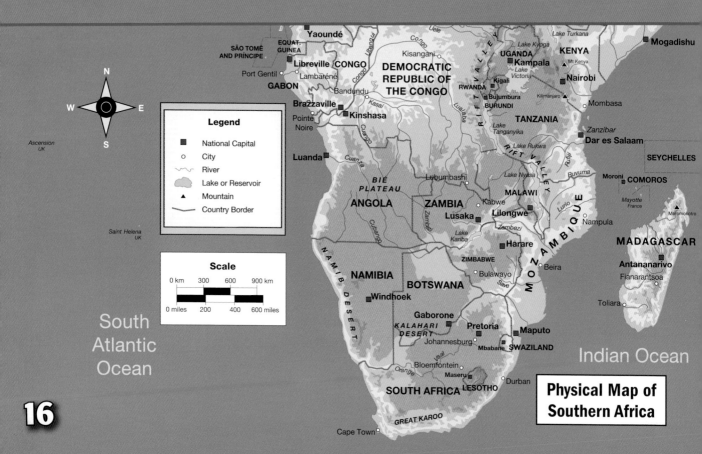

Physical Map of Southern Africa

maps really are. For example, a map's scale bar might say that 1 inch (2.5 cm) on the map is 10 miles (16 km) in real life. You can use this to figure out that if two towns are 4 inches (10 cm) apart on the map, they are really 40 miles (64 km) apart.

The map of South Africa below has a larger scale than the map of southern Africa to the left. This lets you see information that did not fit on the map of the bigger area.

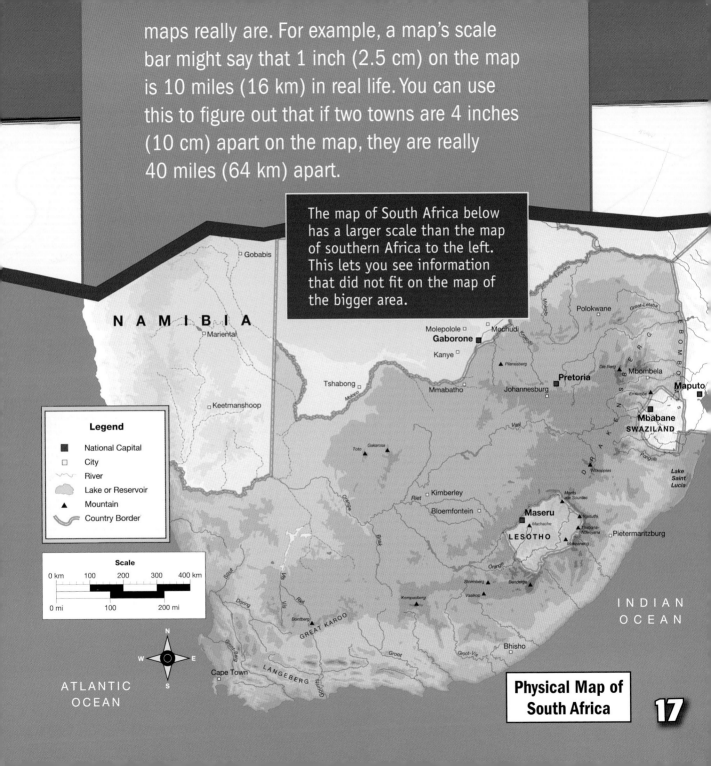

Legend

- ■ National Capital
- □ City
- ∿ River
- Lake or Reservoir
- ▲ Mountain
- Country Border

Scale

0 km 100 200 300 400 km

0 mi 100 200 mi

NAMIBIA

Gobabis

Mariental

Keetmanshoop

Tshabong

Molepolole   Mochudi
Gaborone
Kanye
Mmabatho   Johannesburg

▲ Pilanesberg

Pretoria   Mbombela
Die Berg ▲
Emlembe ▲   **Maputo**

Mbabane
SWAZILAND

Toto ▲   Gakarosa ▲

Witkopples ▲

Lake Saint Lucia

Kimberley

Riet

Bloemfontein   **Maseru**
Machache ▲
LESOTHO
Njesuthi ▲
Thabana-Ntlenyana ▲   Pietermaritzburg
Makoaneng ▲

Monts aux Sources ▲

Orange

Sout   Vis   Riet   Brak

Orange

Stormberg ▲   Bendergie ▲

Kompasberg ▲   Vaalkop ▲

Doring

Bontberg ▲
GREAT KAROO

Groot-Berg   Vis   Gouritz   Groot   Groot-Vis

Bhisho

LANGEBERG

Cape Town

ATLANTIC OCEAN

INDIAN OCEAN

Physical Map of South Africa

17

Topographic Maps

The United States Geological Survey, or USGS, makes **topographic** maps of the United States. Topographic maps are different from other maps. They use line symbols to show how high or low land is. When you look at a topographic map, you can find the highest mountains and deepest valleys.

The topographic map to the right is of Washington's Mount Rainier, above. The loops on the map are contour lines. Every point along a contour line is the same height.

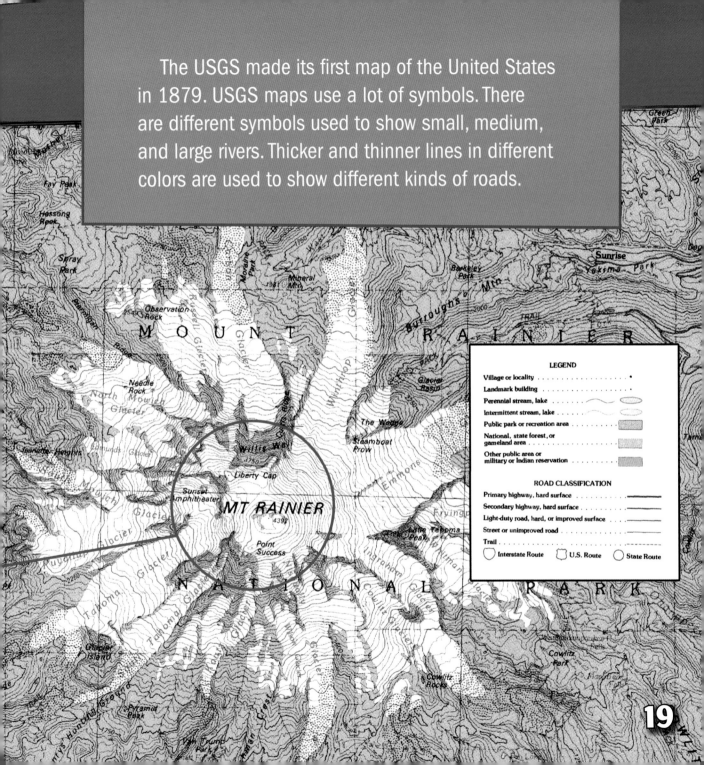

The USGS made its first map of the United States in 1879. USGS maps use a lot of symbols. There are different symbols used to show small, medium, and large rivers. Thicker and thinner lines in different colors are used to show different kinds of roads.

LEGEND

Village or locality . . . . •
Landmark building . . . . ▪
Perennial stream, lake . . . . ⌇ ⬭
Intermittent stream, lake . . . . . . ⌇ ⬭
Public park or recreation area . . . . ▬
National, state forest, or gameland area . . . . ▬
Other public area or military or Indian reservation . . . . ▬

ROAD CLASSIFICATION

Primary highway, hard surface . . . . ▬
Secondary highway, hard surface . . . . ▬
Light-duty road, hard, or improved surface . . . . ▬
Street or unimproved road . . . .
Trail . . . .

⬡ Interstate Route   ⬡ U.S. Route   ◯ State Route

19

The National Park Service makes maps of the national parks in the United States. One of the biggest parks is Yellowstone National Park. It is so big that it is in three states, Montana, Idaho, and Wyoming.

All of the maps made by the National Park Service use the same symbols. Camping grounds are shown with a picture of a tent. Picnic areas are shown with a picture of a picnic table. If you need clean water to drink, look for a picture of a glass of water. Want to go sailing? Look for a picture of a sailboat!

This is part of the National Park Service map of Grand Canyon National Park, in Arizona. Nearly 5 million people visit the park each year.

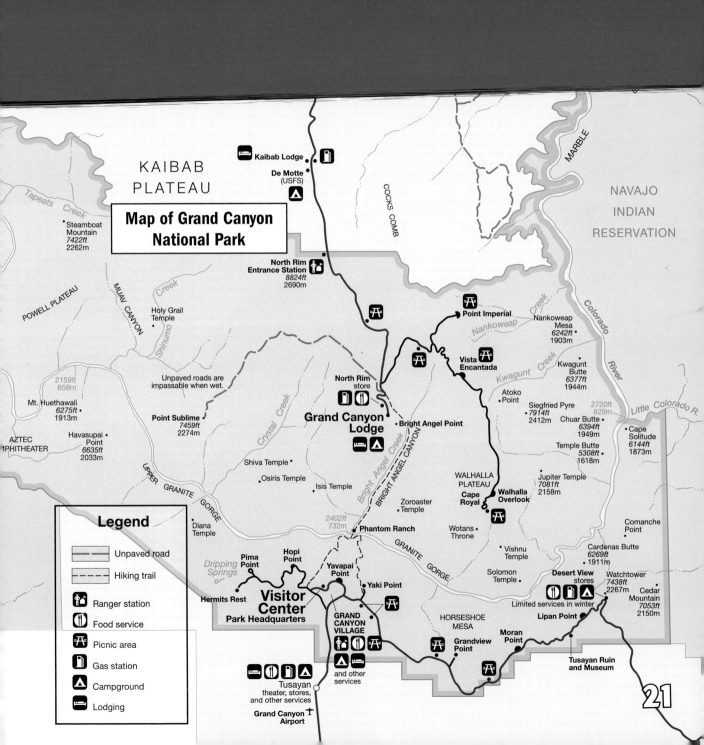

Map of Grand Canyon National Park

KAIBAB PLATEAU

NAVAJO INDIAN RESERVATION

MARBLE

COCKS COMB

Steamboat Mountain
7422ft
2262m

Tapeats Creek

POWELL PLATEAU

MUAV CANYON

Creek

Holy Grail Temple

Shinumo Creek

2159ft
658m

Mt. Huethawali
6275ft
1913m

AZTEC AMPHITHEATER

Havasupai Point
6635ft
2033m

UPPER GRANITE GORGE

Crystal Creek

Shiva Temple

Osiris Temple

Isis Temple

Diana Temple

Dripping Springs

Point Sublime
7459ft
2274m

Unpaved roads are impassable when wet.

🛏 Kaibab Lodge   ⛽
De Motte (USFS)
🔺

North Rim Entrance Station
8824ft
2690m

🔺

🔺

North Rim store
🔋 🍴

Grand Canyon Lodge
🛏 ⛺

Bright Angel Point

Bright Angel Creek

BRIGHT ANGEL CANYON

2402ft
732m

Phantom Ranch

Zoroaster Temple

GRANITE GORGE

Point Imperial

Nankoweap Creek

Vista Encantada 🔺

Atoko Point

WALHALLA PLATEAU

Cape Royal

Walhalla Overlook 🔺

Wotans Throne

Nankoweap Mesa
6242ft
1903m

Kwagunt Creek

Kwagunt Butte
6377ft
1944m

Siegfried Pyre
7914ft
2412m

Chuar Butte
6394ft
1949m

Temple Butte
5308ft
1618m

Jupiter Temple
7081ft
2158m

2720ft
829m

Colorado River

Little Colorado R.

Cape Solitude
6144ft
1873m

Comanche Point

Cardenas Butte
6269ft
1911m

Vishnu Temple

Solomon Temple

Pima Point

Hopi Point

Hermits Rest

Yavapai Point

Yaki Point

Visitor Center
Park Headquarters

🔺

GRAND CANYON VILLAGE
👨 🍴 🔺

⛺ 🛏
and other services

HORSESHOE MESA

🔺

Grandview Point

Moran Point

Desert View stores
🍴 ⛽ ⛺
Limited services in winter

Lipan Point

🔺

Tusayan Ruin and Museum

Watchtower
7438ft
2267m

Cedar Mountain
7053ft
2150m

🛏 🍴 🔋 ⛺
Tusayan theater, stores, and other services

Grand Canyon Airport ✝

Legend

▬▬▬	Unpaved road
- - -	Hiking trail
👨	Ranger station
🍴	Food service
🔺	Picnic area
🔋	Gas station
⛺	Campground
🛏	Lodging

21

Make Your Own Symbols

Keys, legends, and symbols are important tools. They provide useful information and make maps easier to understand. Without them, we would not know which road to take to school!

What symbol would you use to show your house on a map? How about your favorite restaurant? A slide could show where your neighborhood playground is. How about an envelope to show where the post office is? Making your own map symbols can be fun! Remember to make a key or legend so others can understand your map!

When you make a map of a place, you may notice things about it that you had not noticed before. Drawing a map is a great way to learn more about a place.

Glossary

abbreviated (uh-BREE-vee-ayt-ed) Shortened.

biomes (BY-ohmz) Kinds of places with certain weather patterns and kinds of plants.

compass roses (KUM-pus ROHZ-ez) Drawings on maps that show directions.

features (FEE-churz) Special parts.

italics (uh-TA-liks) A kind of writing in which the letters lean to one side.

keys (KEEZ) Boxes on maps that tell what the figures on the maps mean.

legends (LEH-jendz) Boxes on maps that tell what the figures on the maps mean.

population (pop-yoo-LAY-shun) The number of animals or people living in a place.

scale bar (SKAYL BAR) A tool that shows the measurements on a map compared to actual measurements on Earth.

symbols (SIM-bulz) Objects or pictures that stand for something else.

topographic (tah-puh-GRA-fik) Having to do with a type of map that shows different regions, such as mountains, lakes, and forests.

tundra (TUN-druh) The icy land of the coldest parts of the world.

Index

C
cities, 4–5, 7, 9, 12, 14
color(s), 11–14, 19
compass rose(s), 16
countries, 9, 11–12

F
features, 4, 15
fork(s), 7

H
highway(s), 9

I
italics, 15

L
line(s), 8–9, 19

P
people, 4, 13
picture(s), 4, 7, 20

R
restaurant, 7, 22
rivers, 4, 8, 15, 19
road(s), 4, 8, 19, 22

S
scale bar(s), 16–17
star(s), 4, 7
state(s), 9, 11, 20

T
tool(s), 4, 16, 22
tracks, 9
tundra, 12
types, 8, 12

U
United States, 7, 11, 18–20
United States Geological Survey (USGS), 18–19

W
water, 11, 20

Web Sites

Due to the changing nature of Internet links, PowerKids Press has developed an online list of Web sites related to the subject of this book. This site is updated regularly. Please use this link to access the list:
www.powerkidslinks.com/maps/keys/